All About Cats As Pets

All About Cats As Pets

by Marjorie Zaum

Illustrated with photographs

JULIAN MESSNER NEW YORK

Copyright © 1981 by Marjorie Zaum
All rights reserved including the right of
reproduction in whole or in part in any form.
Published by Julian Messner, a Simon & Schuster
Division of Gulf & Western Corporation, Simon &
Schuster Building, 1230 Avenue of the Americas,
New York, N.Y. 10020.

JULIAN MESSNER and colophon are trademarks
of Simon & Schuster, registered in the
U.S. Patent and Trademark Office.

Manufactured in the United States of America

Design by Marjorie Zaum

Library of Congress Cataloging in Publication Data

Zaum, Marjorie.
    All about cats as pets.

    Includes index.
    Summary: Discusses the history and folklore of
cats; their physiology, care, and feeding; cat
language; health problems; toys and games; and
traveling and boarding. Includes lists of plants
and household substances poisonous to cats.
    1. Cats—Juvenile literature. [1. Cats]
I. Title.
SF445.7.Z38   636.8   81-813
ISBN 0-671-33099-3   AACR2

To Mow
the cat I walked away from
and to
dear Mooshie, Gwinevere, and Blackberry

ACKNOWLEDGMENTS

I would like to express my appreciation to my husband, Allan Goldenthal, for his kindness, encouragement, and creative criticism of the
manuscript. I feel grateful to Lee Hoffman, for being, for so many
years, not only a sensitive editor, but a dear friend.

I am indebted to Dr. Louis Camuti, for all that he has taught me
about cats. Dr. Isabel Wright introduced me to the idea (new to me at
the time) that I could have pets and be a responsible pet owner. For
that I thank her deeply, for caring for my pets has brought me great
pleasure.

I especially appreciate the technical advice and guidance given me
by Dr. John Loda and Elizabeth Loda, of the Feline Veterinary
Hospital in Port Washington, New York, and more than that, I want to
thank them for their warm friendship.

Special thanks are due to Dr. John Cave, Medical Director of the
Humane Society of New York, and to Bettina Glaeske, Publicity Direc-
tor, for medical advice and photos. I thank also Dr. Roman
Bohonowych, of the Bide-A-Wee Association of New York, for his
special help and criticism. I want to thank Cindy Burns and Diana
Henley, also of Bide-A-Wee, for their help in providing pictures.

Warm thanks are due to Allan Breznick, Managing Editor of the
ASPCA Publications Dept., for generously contributing both time and
effort in the selection of pictures for this book. Special appreciation to
Sybil Meisel, President of the Pioneers for Animal Welfare Society
(P.A.W.S.), and to all the members, for pictures, criticism of the
manuscript, and personal kindness. Special thanks to Sara Nemerov
for letting me use her picture in this book.

To my dear cats, Lancelot, Minette, Sashie, Rusty, Jennie, and
Bambi, very loud purrs. To May-May, our wonderful German
Shepherd, thanks for taking care of all of us, for loving us, for loving
the cats, and for being such a good dog.

MZ

Contents

Note To The Reader

When you get a new cat or kitten, your first question will probably be: Is it a male or a female? A boy or a girl?

Since all cats are either one or the other, you may wonder why I have used the word "he" throughout this book. I've done so only to make it easier to read, and not because male cats are better or more important than female cats!

So whether your cat is a male or a female, I hope this book will make it easier for you to take care of him or her, and that you and he or she will have happy times together.

MZ

1
Getting to Know Your Cat

BEAUTIFUL, AFFECTIONATE YET INDEPENDENT, YOUR NEW CAT wants to be a true friend and a member of the family. Inside that soft, furry body is an individual capable of feeling love and of being a great companion.

But you must do your part in this friendship and be responsible. This means, first of all, that *your cat is not a toy!* He is a sensitive, living being with needs and feelings very much like your own. He must be fed every single day and given fresh water and a freshly-filled litter pan. He should have a warm place to sleep inside your house. If he is sick, he must be taken to a *veterinarian* (an animal doctor) at once.

Each cat has a different personality. Some are bold and adventurous, while others are sweet and shy. Some cats are always as playful as kittens. Others are quiet and peaceful.

You can help to shape your cat's personality by making sure that he's happy and healthy. Frightened cats can lose their fears and become playful and happy when given love. Nervous cats simmer down and become affectionate when treated with kindness.

Even though cats are home-loving creatures, they seem to remember that they were born free. Cats are independent and

Lancelot is a bold, adventurous cat. *(Photo by Marjorie Zaum)*

Mooshie is a shy, quiet cat. *(Photo by Marjorie Zaum)*

very rarely do tricks, as dogs will, to please people. If you want to pet or play with your cat when he doesn't feel like it, he'll simply walk away. Cats respect themselves and their own wishes, and cat owners learn to admire their pet's spirit of independence.

A kitten should be given the same tender, loving care as any new baby. Let your kitten play and romp, but don't let him get overtired. Eating, sleeping, and playing are what kittens want to do. Older cats may be quieter, but they still love playing games. Never allow anyone to handle your kitten or cat roughly.

Never hit or shout at a cat. This will not train him, but it *will* damage your friendship. Most cats will not obey commands as dogs do. They learn by cooperation. Your cat has to be interested

A kitten should be treated gently. *(Photo courtesy of The Humane Society of New York)*

in what you want him to do and willing to learn the rules for living in your house.

Cats are *nocturnal* (active at night). Usually they take long naps during the day and go exploring at night. Climbing high, discovering secret hiding places, and sniffing things are fun for your cat.

Many cats like to sleep with people whom they love. They like warmth, coziness, soft chairs, pillows, and blankets. Some people give their cats clean, soft towels to sleep on and to keep for their own.

Cats often sleep with people that they love. *(Photo by Rev. Arlyn J. Hausman, courtesy of the ASPCA Education Dept.)*

Cats like to perch in high places. If you can, clear off the top of a cabinet or high shelf so your cat can have a place of his own. There he can nap, feel comfortable and safe, and watch the human world from above.

Talk to your cat, watch him, and learn cat language. Cats communicate with us by using their voices, eyes, and bodies. From the different positions of their ears, whiskers, tails, and general body posture, you can understand much of what your cat feels and is trying to tell you.

Rusty likes to sit on this special shelf built for him. It is up high so he can feel comfortable. *(Photo by Allan Goldenthal)*

Learn to know your cat and his ways. Love him for what he is and don't expect him to act like a dog or a human. Make your cat's life a pleasure and he'll be a pleasure to you.

The word cat is similar in many languages of the world.

Arab-*Kitt*	Italian-*Gatto*
Armenian-*Kitta*	Latin-*Catta*
Chinese-*Mow**	Nubian-*Kadiska*
Dutch-*Kot*	Polish-*Kot*
Egyptian-*Mau**	Russian-*Kot*
French-*Chat*	Spanish-*Gato*
German-*Katze*	Turkish-*Kati*
Irish-*Pus*	Welsh-*Cath*

*The Chinese *Mow* and the Egyptian *Mau* imitate the sound a cat makes. *(Photo courtesy of The Humane Society of New York)*

2
History and Folklore

LONG BEFORE HUMANS WALKED UPON THE EARTH, *MIACIS,* ancestor of the cat, roamed the primeval forests and lived in the treetops. Miacis had a long body, a long tail, short legs, and probably *retractable claws*—claws that could be extended or pulled in at will. Scientists think that Miacis was also the ancestor of the dog, bear, weasel, fox, and raccoon.

Dinictis, who looked more like today's cat, appeared about thirty million years ago. Dinictis was a fast-moving, *carnivorous* (flesh-eating) animal, intelligent and strong. His teeth were designed for stabbing and tearing. With his strong muscular legs, he was able to spring upon animals larger than himself. Dinictis had the equipment to survive in a primitive, competitive world.

Our present-day cat, whose scientific name is *Felis,* evolved from Dinictis. It became a domestic pet only about four or five thousand years ago.

The first records of cats were kept by the ancient Egyptians. They admired cats and treated them with great respect. The cat was thought to be sacred to the Egyptian goddess Isis (sometimes called Bast or Mut).

The Egyptians were hard-working farm people. They stored

15

Cats were a favorite subject of Egyptian artists. Many museums have Egyptian sections where you can see sculptures carved from precious stones. This drawing was made from an ancient Egyptian bronze sculpture. *(Drawing by Marjorie Zaum)*

their grain in granaries. Cats were put there to kill the rodents that would have eaten the grain. Poisonous snakes were found on many farms, and cats killed these, also.

The Egyptians loved their cats. House cats were treasured. If one was sick, he was tended with great care. If a family's cat died, he was *embalmed* (treated with a chemical preservative), *mummified* (made ready for burial) and buried with the same ceremony given to humans. To kill a cat was a crime punishable by death.

Later, when the Roman armies conquered the known world, they brought their cats with them on their marches. Many Roman soldiers had pictures of cats embroidered on their banners and painted on their shields. And because of its independent nature, the cat was a symbol of liberty to the Romans.

But cats were not treated so well everywhere. During the Middle Ages (476 A.D. to 1453) in Europe, superstitious people believed that cats were witches and could do harm. Many cats suffered terrible punishments because of this ignorant belief.

There are stories about cats and their wonderful qualities that come from every country in the world. One French story tells of a black cat who showed people the way to wealth. When the cat was taken to a place where five roads met and then let go, he would choose the road that led to hidden treasure.

In a Nordic legend, Freya, the sun goddess, traveled all over the countryside in a chariot drawn by two cats. Farmers who left saucers of milk in their cornfields for her cats were given her blessing. Their harvests received special protection.

The Chinese believed that cats had the power to drive away evil spirits, and a cat spirit was worshipped in certain parts of China. Cats were also used to protect silkworms against rats.

In sixth-century Japan, sacrifices were made to the "Guardian of the Manuscripts." This was a sacred cat whose responsibility was to guard the temple scrolls against mice and rats.

The colonists brought their cats with them to the New World. Cats performed the same jobs on the colonial farms and in the towns as they had in Europe. After the day's work was done, the colonial cat sat close to the fireplace, enjoying its warmth with the rest of the family.

The hard-working cat has a long history of helping people and of being a close companion to humans.

3
Your Cat's Basic Needs

YOUR CAT HAS A FEW SIMPLE BUT BASIC NEEDS. HE MUST HAVE food, water, litter, and medical care when necessary.

A kitten needs a little more time and attention than an older cat. He is a baby, and his future health and happiness depend on the care you give him now.

The first few days in your house should be peaceful and quiet. Your kitten or cat has just gone through an awful experience. He was probably taken away from his warm mother and litter mates and shut in a dark, cat carrier.

The older cat may have been taken from a shelter, a pet shop, or found abandoned in the street. After a bumpy ride in the carrier, he was released into a strange, unknown world—your house. All the new sights, sounds, and odors can frighten him. He needs time to get used to his new home.

Open the carrier in a quiet room where your cat or kitten can stay for the first few days. Soothe him with gentle petting and speak to him in a soft voice. Bring in his food, water, and a filled litter pan. (See page 23.)

Anyone who gets a new cat or kitten naturally wants to hold him and hug him right away. Since their personalities are so different, one cat may jump right into your lap, while another may hide under furniture.

If your cat is shy, leave him alone for a short time. Later, when you come in the room, put a little food in a dish near him. This may help to coax him out if he is hiding. Let him eat quietly. If you think he's tired, let him sleep. Show him kind behavior so he will know you're friendly and won't hurt him.

Above all, don't grab. Let him come to you. Put your hand out, palm up, for him to sniff. If you want to hold him, put one hand on his chest under his front legs. Put your other hand under his rear parts, making a little seat for him. Hold him so that he is

This boy is learning to hold his cat correctly. *(Photo by Anne F. Jarvis, courtesy of the ASPCA Education Dept.)*

facing outward. Never put your face close to the face of a new or frightened cat. And don't carry him by the scruff of the neck or let his hind legs dangle.

Have you thought of a name for your cat? Choose one that is simple to say and fits his personality. Names with two syllables are easier for your cat to recognize. Teach him his name by calling him and giving him a reward and praise when he comes. Use his name while petting him, when feeding him, and whenever you speak to him.

Lifting a cat.
(Bide-A-Wee
photo by Susan Brooks)

Never use his name when you want him to stop doing something. This will confuse him. Simply say "stop" or "no" in a firm voice. Answering to his name should mean only good things for him.

Where will your cat sleep? You can make a bed for him out of a cardboard carton. It should have high sides to protect him from drafts. Cut down one side so he can get in and out easily, especially if he's a kitten. Lining the carton with clean, soft towels will make it very comfortable. But there is no guarantee that your

Angel sleeps with Grandma on very cold nights.   *(Photo by Kenneth Holder, courtesy of the ASPCA Education Dept.)*

Sybil enjoys a nap in the laundry basket. *(Photo courtesy of Pioneers for Animal Welfare Society—P.A.W.S.)*

cat will use it! As cats get older, they like to find their own sleeping places. Most cats find that a favorite chair, your bed, or on top of your clothes are good places to sleep.

Your cat needs a plastic litter pan and litter. You need a special slotted spoon. Litter is ground clay which absorbs moisture and odor. Litter, the pan, and the special spoon for handling litter can be bought in department stores, supermarkets, or pet shops.

With the slotted spoon, remove solid waste from the tray

every day. Stir the damp litter around so it can dry. Change the litter at least once a week and wash the pan with a mild detergent and hot water. Rinse out all the soap.

Keep the litter pan in your bathroom if you have room there. When no one is using the bathroom, leave the door slightly open so your cat can go in and out. If there is no room in your bathroom for the litter pan, find a place for it that is easy for your cat to reach. It should not be put outside the house.

Show your cat where the litter pan is. Most older cats know the use of the litter pan as soon as they are put in it. But a kitten may need a little training.

After your kitten has eaten, put him in the pan and wait. If he doesn't want to use the pan, try again after the next meal.

Put a layer of litter in the bottom of the cat's pan about 2½ inches deep.

When your kitten has used the pan, don't remove the waste or change the litter right away. Let the kitten get the scent so he can remember the purpose of the litter pan.

(If your cat goes to the litter pan again and again and strains or cries, or frequently urinates outside the pan, or if there is blood in the urine, he is sick and you should call your veterinarian at once.)

A scratching post is not a toy for your cat. He needs it to sharpen his claws and stretch his body. The post should be tall and have a solid base so it won't fall over when your cat leans his full weight against it.

Left: A carpet-covered scratching post with a catnip toy attached to it. Right: A log scratching post.

Train your cat to use his post. If you see him scratching furniture, say "no" firmly. Pick him up and bring him to his post. Place his paws on it and make a scratching motion with them. Do this patiently each time you see him scratching furniture until he learns. Make the post more attractive to him by rubbing some catnip (see page 39) on it. Scratching posts are sold in department stores and pet supply shops.

Your cat's equipment—food dish, water bowl, scratching post, and especially his litter pan—should not be moved around to different places. Once you've decided where to put these things, leave them there so your cat can easily find them.

Grooming, which means brushing and combing the loose hairs from your cat's coat, helps to prevent *hairballs.* (See page 79.)

Jojo likes to be groomed when he's just waking up from a nap. *(Bide-A-Wee photo by Susan Brooks)*

Use a small plastic comb or a small brush, or both. At first, most cats try to play with the brush and comb, so let him see and sniff them. Take him on your lap or sit on the floor with him. With his back to you, gently comb the top of his head and work your way down his back with short strokes. Do this for only a minute or two several times a day until your cat gets used to it.

Don't force or hold him against his will. Grooming should be a pleasure for him, not an ordeal. A slightly sleepy cat usually takes to grooming better than one who feels frisky. Long-haired cats need to be groomed every day. Don't bathe your cat unless your veterinarian has told you to do so.

Your cat should be brought to a veterinarian within the first few days after you get him. He will give your cat an examination and shots against *pneumonitis* and *feline distemper.*

Ask people who have cats if they can recommend a veterinarian. Or you and your parents can go to an animal hospital where veterinarians are on the staff. Your local humane society may have a clinic where animals are treated. Animal hospitals, veterinarians, and humane societies are listed in the yellow pages of your phone book.

A cat may have an emergency at night or on a weekend when the veterinarian is not in his office. You or your parents should ask him what to do in case this happens. He may give you a special number to call or he may give you the name of an animal hospital that has a 24-hour schedule. Make a note of the information and keep it where you can easily find it.

Take your pet to the veterinarian in a cat carrier. If you carry him, he may get frightened, jump out of your arms, and run away. Cat carriers are usually made of fiberboard and open from the top so your cat can be put inside. The carrier has holes for air and usually a screen in the front. Your cat can see out, but he is safe inside. Get one that is big enough for him to sit in comfortably. Remember that a kitten will grow larger. Carriers are sold in pet shops and department stores.

Cats are so intelligent that many people think they can take care of themselves. They can't. Your cat needs you to give him the care and attention he needs.

Suzie and Theresa take their cats to the veterinarian. *(Photo by Martin Rubinstein, courtesy of Pioneers for Animal Welfare Society—P.A.W.S.)*

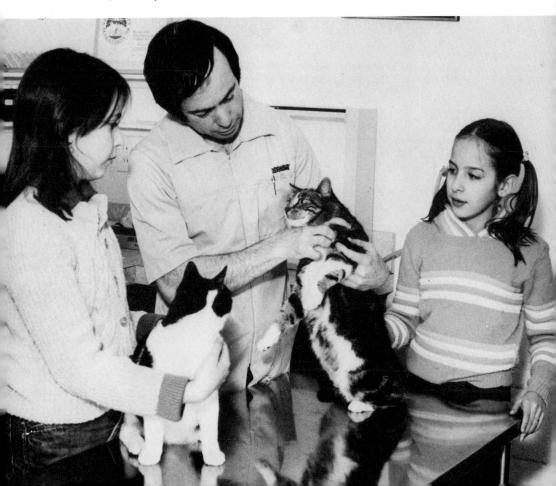

4
Safety First

SOON YOUR CAT WILL BE READY TO EXPLORE THE WHOLE HOUSE or apartment. Most people don't know that every house has things in it which are harmful for cats. And no cat really has nine lives.

You can make your house safe for your pet by removing things which are dangerous for him. A cat, like a baby, may eat or drink something that he finds around the house and get very sick. A list of substances poisonous for cats is on page 91. These things must be kept where your cat can't get them.

Insecticide spray, which is used in houses to get rid of bugs, can make your cat very sick. Keep him away from rooms that have been sprayed for several hours until the rooms are completely aired out.

Some cats chew the leaves of house plants. Many of the leaves are poisonous or have been sprayed with poisonous insecticide. House plants can be transferred to hanging pots and placed too high for your cat to reach. A list of poisonous plants is on page 90.

Cats lick off and swallow things that stick to their fur. If what is on the cat's fur is poisonous—such as household cleaners like ammonia—the cat will poison himself by licking his fur.

Sewing supplies, like needles, pins, or thread, should not be

Becky is about to taste a flower. It might be poisonous or have been sprayed with a poisonous insecticide. *(Photo by Rebecca Bollerman, courtesy of the ASPCA Education Dept.)*

left where your cat might sit or step on them. Swallowed thread is dangerous because it can get wound around his intestines.

Small things that may be swallowed, and objects with sharp edges, are dangerous and shouldn't be left where your cat can find them. Don't let him play with any of the following things:

buttons	scissors	ribbons
marbles	razor blades	plastic wrap
pins, needles	knives	aluminum foil
safety pins	matches	cellophane
staples	bottle caps	string
paper clips	rubber bands	thread
tacks, nails	hairpins, bobby pins	yarn or balls of yarn

Lancelot felt like sitting in the roasting pan, but it is dangerous for him to be near the stove. If he decides to chew bits of the aluminum foil in the pan, he can get very sick. *(Photo by Marjorie Zaum)*

If you buy him a stuffed toy, remove the glass eyes and other decorations.

Christmas can be a very sad time for kittens and cats that have been given to children as gifts. Cats play with Christmas trees, pine needles, glass ornaments, tinsel, fiberglass snow, holly leaves, and berries. These can all be chewed and swallowed, and therefore they are all dangerous. Your cat may sit on tinsel, lick it off his fur, and swallow it. The results can be disastrous. Serious illness can result for these Christmas cats and, of course, for the cat you may already have. So if you receive a cat or kitten for Christmas, or if you already have a cat, be sure he's never alone in a room with Christmas decorations.

Valuable or breakable objects should be put away for awhile, especially if you have a kitten. Cats are sure-footed, but even the most careful one may misjudge and take a false step. If he breaks something, he's not a bad cat. It was an accident that is embarrassing to him.

If glass breaks, clean it up. If it is on a rug, vacuum it. (If you can't run a vacuum cleaner by yourself, ask an adult to help you.) If it is on the floor, wipe it up with a thick wad of wet paper towels. Be sure you get every bit of glass. Don't allow your cat near the area until the glass, or a spill which could be dangerous to him, is all cleaned up.

Cupboard and closet doors should be tightly closed. If not, your cat will probably go inside to explore and play. Someday you may spend hours searching for your cat only to find that he was fast asleep in a closet all the time.

Make sure that outside doors are shut and windows screened. Windows without screens must be kept closed. Cats love to sit on windowsills, and sooner or later they want to explore outside. A cat can also fall out of a window and be seriously hurt or killed.

When you take a cat into your house, he is a house pet. He should not go outside. The street is dangerous for cats. They may be hit by a car, eat garbage, pick up diseases, or produce kittens that no one wants. Cats that are let out of apartment houses hardly ever find their way home, if they survive at all.

Cats roaming around in the country can get caught in traps. They, too, may catch diseases and produce kittens that no one

The window was screened, but Lancelot wiggled through the small opening and hung by his claws to a window ledge twelve stories high. He was rescued and the opening was covered with additional screening to prevent this from happening again.
(Photo by Marjorie Zaum)

cares about. Animal shelters are overcrowded with unwanted kittens and cats. Their chances for adoption are very small.

Never take your cat out of the house in your arms, even for a minute. In that minute, a street noise or sudden movement may frighten him and he may jump away from you and get lost in the street. Always put him in his carrier before you leave the house.

Take a few precautions in the beginning and you won't have problems later on. And keep your cat safe by keeping him home.

DO'S and DON'T'S

DON'T allow your cat near a flame on the kitchen stove or near a fireplace without a screen.

DON'T allow your cat near an electric fan.

DON'T close refrigerator, closet, drawers, or cupboard doors without checking to see if your cat is inside!

DO cover garbage pails tightly.

DO keep the lid of the toilet closed to prevent your cat from drinking the water in the toilet bowl.

DO keep all medicines in a closed cabinet that your cat can't open.

DO ask friends and family, when entering and leaving your house, to close outside doors quickly to prevent your cat from darting out and getting lost.

DO remember that your pet's life is much shorter than yours, so make his days happy ones and enjoy yourselves together.

Frannie's owners made this special seat so she can look out through the screen door. *(Photo by Richard Franzen, courtesy of the ASPCA Education Dept.)*

5
Feeding Your Cat

A HEALTHY CAT ENJOYS AND LOOKS FORWARD TO MEALTIMES. These are important events in his day. The familiar sound of the opening of a can or the cupboard door where catfood is kept will bring your cat rushing to you from wherever he is.

Since he is your cat, you should be the one to feed him at the same times every day. Once you have a regular routine, he'll come at the time he expects to be fed, to remind you in case you should be slow or late.

Your cat needs a dish for food and a bowl for water. The feeding dishes should not be cracked or dirty. Place them where your cat will not be stepped on or interfered with while he is eating. Both the dish and the water bowl should be heavy enough so that he can't tip them over. After every meal, wash the dish thoroughly with hot water. Don't use soap or detergent. They can leave unpleasant traces on the dish that your cat can smell and taste.

Your cat needs a balanced diet. Table scraps, leftovers, and dogfood are not good for him.

Ask the veterinarian how old your kitten is, for kittens that have been taken away from their mothers before they are six weeks old are considered orphans. Here is a chart that will help in feeding your kitten.

34

Kitten Feeding Chart

Kittens under six weeks (orphans):

Feed: Kitten milk replacer (available from your veterinarian or from pet shops), cottage cheese, baby cereals, milk. When your kitten is over three weeks he can also have strained-meat baby foods—beef, chicken, or lamb.

Quantity: As much as he wants to eat.

Number of meals: Feed four to six times a day. Very small kittens should be fed every three to four hours. You will have to bottle-feed your kitten until he is three to four weeks old. At this age he can begin to lap milk from a saucer. Wet your finger in the milk and put it to your kitten's lips. When he begins to suck your finger, gently lower his head so that his lips touch the milk at the edge of the dish.

Kittens over six weeks:

Feed: Kitten chow with water. Milk, cottage cheese, baby cereals, and strained-meat baby foods can be given. Ask your veterinarian about a vitamin/mineral supplement.

Quantity: As much as your kitten wants. They usually eat their fill in ten or fifteen minutes.

Number of meals: Feed four times a day. Gradually decrease the number of meals so that when your kitten is three months old, he gets two main meals a day and perhaps a small third meal.

Kittens over three months:

Feed: Main diet can be kitten chow and water. For variety, add cottage cheese, cooked egg, strained-meat baby foods, and soft, moist foods. You may also give small amounts of canned food, but withdraw this if your kitten has loose bowel movements.

Quantity: He can eat as much as he wants.

Number of meals: Feed two main meals a day. Leave extra food out so he can eat whenever he is hungry.

Kittens over six months:

Feed: Some canned food, some cat chow, and soft, moist foods. Any table food that is good for him. (See page 37.) Cottage cheese, cooked egg.

Quantity: Canned food — one can (about six ounces) a day. Dry food — follow feeding instructions on the package.

Number of meals: Two a day.

A motherless kitten must be bottle fed.
(Photo by Carroll Ries, courtesy of the ASPCA Education Dept.)

A cat is an adult at one year old. He can be given canned, semi-moist, and dry food. Look for labels that say "complete, balanced diet." Buy only well-known brands of cat food and feed your cat a variety of flavors. He should eat about one can (six ounces) of food a day. If you give him semi-moist or dry food, follow the feeding instructions on the package. The total amount of food can be divided into two or three meals a day.

The best diet is probably a combination of canned food with semi-moist or canned food with dry. Some veterinarians think that a diet of dry food alone may cause *cystitis* (see page 79). Cats who have had cystitis, especially male cats, should not eat dry food at all.

Add a teaspoonful of ordinary corn oil to the food two or three times a week. This will increase the fat content of his diet. Left over pieces of cooked animal fat can be given as a supplement.

After the body has taken all it needs from the foods we eat, there is sometimes a leftover part called *ash* that the body cannot use. Some doctors think that a high ash content in cats' food causes them to become ill. So until we are sure, it's safer to buy foods that are low (3% or less) in ash content.

The ash content of canned food is usually listed on the back of the can in very small print. In dry food, the ash content may be higher, but you can buy a special brand of dry food with a low ash content in pet supply stores.

Read the labels on the cans and know what you are giving your cat. Don't let him get hooked on one favorite food that he likes best. Different foods will give him the balance he needs in his diet.

Foods that have beef, liver, chicken, turkey, kidney, heart, eggs, and cheese in them are good for cats. They should not eat

The actress Sandy Dennis has a large cat family to feed. *(Photo by Lynn Karlin, courtesy of the ASPCA Education Dept.)*

ham or pork. Most cats like tuna, but it is *not* good for them as a steady diet. Combinations, like tuna and egg or salmon and liver, can be fed once a week as a treat.

Other foods that cats may have, in addition to their basic diets, are small amounts of cottage cheese, cream cheese, egg yolk beaten up in milk, and non-starchy vegetables. Adult cats don't need milk as a regular part of their diet, and it has a laxative effect on some cats.

Never give your cat chicken bones or any other bones. They can splinter and the sharp pieces could pierce his throat or stomach. Don't give raw meat or fish. Poultry skin, starchy or highly-seasoned foods are also bad for him.

Serve food at room temperature, not ice-cold. Catfood left in the refrigerator overnight should be warmed before giving it to your cat. If you leave canned food out overnight, it may be spoiled by morning. Throw these leftovers away.

If your cat has stopped eating for more than two days, check him for symptoms (see chapter 11) and call your veterinarian.

Cats don't drink a lot of water. Nevertheless, it should be left out for them at all times. Change the water often. It's unpleasant and unhealthy to drink water that is dusty or has been in the bowl for days.

Decide when and how many meals a day you will give your cat and keep to that schedule. It's a good idea to feed your cat his meals just before you have yours so he doesn't have to wait hungrily while you eat.

Catnip is a wonderful treat. It is sold in supermarkets and pet shops. To give catnip, place a paper towel on the floor and put about one-quarter teaspoon of it in the center. It will make your cat feel excited and playful. He will sniff, eat, and roll around in it. (*Don't* give it to a cat who is ill.) Keep the catnip in a closed box or plastic container.

Other treats you might buy are strained or junior all-meat baby foods. Some people keep dry food to use as a treat, if it isn't the cat's main diet.

Use common sense in feeding your pet. Don't think that you can stuff him with food and treats one day to make up for having forgotten to feed him the day before! Make his meals nutritious, regular, and pleasant. A healthy cat, with a shining coat and glowing eyes, is a happy cat. And you, as a responsible person, will be proud of your cat's well-being.

"Hurry up! I'm starving!" *(Photo courtesy of The Humane Society of New York)*

6
Cat Language

YOUR CAT WILL TRY TO LEARN WHAT YOUR SOUNDS AND GESTURES mean. To have a real friendship with him, it's important for you to learn what his sounds and gestures mean—to learn cat language. They express their language with their voices, eyes, ears, whiskers, tails, and bodies.

Body language is a phrase you may have heard before. It is usually used to describe the meanings of human body positions. Cats, of course, use body language all the time to communicate among themselves, people, and other animals.

Your cat's meow of greeting, his meow of hunger, or several meows in a longer message will be in various tones. Cats can make many other sounds besides "meow." If you listen carefully, you may be able to hear sounds like "mrooo" or "mrrow," and many others. Experts have counted up to 100 different sounds that cats can make.

When your cat speaks, answer him. You'll understand each other better if you have many conversations. Tell him where you're going and when you're coming back. He'll understand much of what you are saying from your body language and from your tone of voice.

The purr shows happiness and contentment. Sometimes it

Brenda and Pavlova have a deep understanding between them.
(Photo by Lee Bryant, courtesy of the ASPCA Education Dept.)

cannot be heard, but if you put your hand on your cat's throat, you will feel its vibrations. A few cats purr when they are in pain. No one knows why they do this. It may be a way of comforting themselves when they are sick.

The hiss and the growl can express feelings from slight annoyance to real anger. A cat may "yowl" if accidentally stepped on. You know what this means. But a cat making a yowling, whining sound to another cat is angry and may be preparing for a fight. Separate them until they calm down.

Nursing is the kitten's first pleasure in life. It is connected with food, warmth, and protection. A cat pushing his front paws up and down on your lap or on anything soft is showing the happy, contented feeling of this first pleasure. This motion, called *kneading*, is done by adult cats when they are extremely happy.

A cat who loves you will often rub or bump his head, tail, or entire body against you. Because the cat's touch and his gestures are often gentle and light, some people don't pay any attention to them. A cat who is ignored can certainly feel he's not wanted and soon will stop caring about his owner at all.

The mother cat licks and washes her kittens soon after they are born. When your cat licks your hand or face, it's a sign of affection, like a kiss. A cat licking himself shows a feeling of pride

Julie and Susan know that Fluffer is petting Susan with his tail.
(Photo courtesy of Rev. Robert Van Gorder and Virginia Chapman)

and happiness. Cats also lick and wash other cats whom they love.

Sometimes cats lick themselves when confused or embarrassed. This is done with quick, short licks and is not the same as grooming or washing.

Cats usually wash their paws after meals. This, too, expresses a feeling of contentment.

There is a fable about why cats wash their paws after eating that was told by Aesop, a famous Greek storyteller, who lived about 2,600 years ago. It happened that Cat had caught Bird and was preparing to eat him for dinner. Holding Bird down with one paw, Cat leaned over intending to take his first bite. Bird, who was very clever, said, "Cat, what crude manners you have. How uncouth you are!"

Cat, who prided himself on his elegant taste and good manners, was very offended. "What do you mean?" he demanded.

"Why," said clever Bird, "everyone knows that animals with clean habits and graceful manners wash their paws before dinner!"

Cat, who considered himself the cleanest, most graceful of creatures, immediately lifted the paw that was holding Bird and began to wash. Bird flew away, chirping and laughing.

Cat had learned his lesson, and to this day washes his paws after dinner, lest the dinner fly away.

The cat's tail can tell you a great deal about his mood. Held high, straight up, sometimes with a little curl at the tip, he's feeling fine. The tail held straight out in a horizontal position means he's stalking or on business of his own. Don't interfere. A fast lashing back and forth of the tail shows anger. If, at the same time, the pupils of his eyes are very round and his eyes appear dark, he's

Patrick's tail indicates that, "I feel fine." *(Photo courtesy of The Humane Society of New York)*

very angry! Try to put him in a room by himself and stay away until he is calmer. A tail hanging down and droopy means your cat is disappointed. A gently waving tail means he is pleased.

A cat can bush out the fur on his tail and coat until he actually looks twice his normal size. If you see this happen, it means that your cat has been badly frightened by something and is trying to look terrifying to his enemy.

A cat's ears normally point straight up. Ears pointed forward show curiosity. Ears that are held flat against his head mean that

Bridget is listening to sounds that are very far away. *(Photo courtesy of The Humane Society of New York)*

he's frightened or angry. Some cats point their ears in opposite directions when puzzled. At times they seem to be listening very intently to faraway sounds that we can't hear. Loud, harsh sound is very upsetting to them. Some cats seem to like music, even though they probably hear all the scratches on a record.

If you're talking about your cat and his ears and tail twitch, you can be sure he knows you're talking about him.

Eyes kept almost closed show contentment. The almost-closed position is sometimes said to be the smile of the cat. A series

His almost-closed eyes show that Lancelot feels happy. *(Photo by Marjorie Zaum)*

of eyeblinks shows trust, happiness, and that your cat likes your company. Return the compliment and blink back. Never try to out-stare a cat, for staring sometimes precedes a fight between animals. He may think you are threatening him.

Paws are also used to communicate. A brisk little tap with his front paw often means "Don't." Your cat is teaching you in the same way his mother taught and guided him. His claws will not be extended, but if you don't pay attention to the warning paw, they may be next time. Some cats use their paws to pet you. Some will even hold your arm or leg with their front legs and paws, as though begging you not to leave. If you're eating something that smells delicious to your cat, he may tap you several times. This means, "I want some!"

Kicking back sand with the front or hind legs is the way cats cover waste when they're in the litter pan. They use this movement to express a dislike for their dinner, or anything else that they don't like.

Deedee does not want his owner to go away.
(Photo by K.H. Danskin, courtesy of the ASPCA Education Dept.)

Tests made at the Institute for the Study of Animal Problems in Washington, D.C. showed that cats and dogs, like people, are either right-handed or left-handed. That is, they favor either their right or left paws.

Whiskers extended to their full span show curiosity and alertness. Droopy whiskers can mean boredom or illness. Whiskers extended from mouth to ear, held flat against the face, is another way your cat "smiles."

If your cat dances sideways with his body slightly arched, taking little leaps, he is inviting you to play. If he suddenly stops playing and crouches, he is tired or frightened. Stop the game and reassure him. Use a soft tone of voice and tell him you were only playing.

Besides the cat language common to all cats, each cat has his own special ways of communicating.

Some cat owners feel that they and their cats have another kind of communication known as ESP, or extra-sensory perception. People and cats who have lived together and have been close friends for a long time sometimes develop this ability to understand each other without words or gestures.

Think about what your sounds and body movements may mean to your cat. Sudden, abrupt gestures, loud yelling, wild running around, or running after him can upset or frighten him, even if you do these things while playing. He doesn't know this for sure. Most cats just don't like a racket.

To greet someone with affection and be ignored or to be in pain and unable to ask for help are some of the reasons why it is important to understand what our pets are trying to tell us.

7
Toys and Games

CATS NEED TOYS AND GAMES TO KEEP THEM HAPPY AND ACTIVE.
Playing games with your cat will be fun for both of you. Using your cat as a thing for your own amusement, without thought for his welfare, is wrong. People who use their cats this way should not have cats.

When you play with your cat, never make your hand a toy. Don't wiggle your fingers or make fast motions. Your cat, happy to play and excited, may reach out and grab you with his sharp claws. He will think this is all part of the game. Train your cat to use toys that you give him and in that way you won't risk being scratched.

Toys should be simple and safe. Soft knitted balls, stuffed toys, and plastic balls are all good. A carton filled with crumpled tissue paper can delight your cat for hours. Cats love crawling into paper bags and climbing into empty cartons. Cartons should be clean and not have staples or anything in them that could hurt your cat.

You can make an ordinary grocery bag more interesting by cutting eye holes in the sides of the bag. A cat in a bag thinks you can't see him, even though his tail may be outside the bag. He'll

A soft, knitted ball is lots of fun. *(Bide-a-Wee photo by Susan Brooks)*

Lancelot likes playing
and snoozing in a
carton filled with
crumpled tissue paper.
(Photo by Marjorie Zaum)

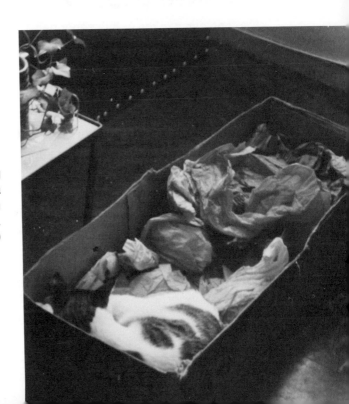

"No one can see me in this paper bag." *(Photo by ASPCA, courtesy of the Newspaper National Snapshot Awards)*

come dashing out when you least expect him.

If you have an old, clean sock you can use it to make a toy. Be sure that it has no holes or tears in it. Fill the foot part with a handful of catnip and tie a strong knot in the middle of the sock so the catnip won't fall out. (This is a good way to use one sock when the other of the pair is lost!)

Tennis balls or plastic eggs are other good toys. When you roll a ball or an egg for your cat to chase, do it in a clear area so he won't be confused by a lot of objects or people. When he pounces on the ball, be sure to praise him. Most cats will want you to throw or roll the ball many times.

Cats also like toys that they can bat. Tie a soft ball to the end of a string and wave the string back and forth. He'll try to bat the ball and jump up after it. Don't let him get wound up or chew the string as that is dangerous for him.

If your cat suddenly stops playing, you stop, too, for he may be tired or frightened.

Cats, especially kittens, love to watch water dripping from faucets. They love seeing dishes washed, so, if this is one of your

"I think I'll have a drink." *(Photo by Karen Ault, courtesy of the ASPCA Education Dept.)*

jobs, having your cat for company will make it easier.

Chasing a cat makes no sense. He will be running away from you and that's not a game. Roll his ball, or his soft toy, or something he can run after and catch.

Never ignore your cat's invitation to play. If you're busy and can't stop what you're doing, tell him you will play later. Don't let his toys get lost or thrown all over the house. Gather them up at night and put them in an uncovered box. He can take them out of the box and play by himself when you're not there.

Kittens are usually more active than older cats, but older cats still love games. They are creative and can invent games of their own. They enjoy climbing, exploring, and just sitting and watching you or the scene outside the window.

As time goes on, you'll learn more about the games your cat likes and the games he's trying to teach you.

Gwinny enjoys watching the family. *(Photo by Marjorie Zaum)*

8
Cats and Cats, Cats and Dogs, and Cats and Babies

FOR SOME TIME NOW, YOU HAVE BEEN THE PROUD OWNER OF ONE cat. Suddenly, you may become the proud owner of two!

It can happen in different ways. You may go to a shelter and adopt a second cat because you feel your first cat is lonely. Or a friend's cat has had a litter of kittens and you're begged to take one because the family can't keep all of them. Or on some cold, rainy afternoon when you're walking home from school, a little cat darts out of the bushes, runs up to you and cries!

"I'm cold, wet, hungry, and alone in the world! Please take me home!" he seems to be saying. What can you do? You already have a cat. But it is certainly possible for you, your family, and two cats to live together happily.

If you have adopted a second cat from a shelter, he will probably be given his shots there. If not, he must be taken to a veterinarian for his shots.

If you've taken in a stray, keep him apart from your first cat. You must protect the cat at home because you don't know if the stray is sick or well. You must be sure that the cat you have found doesn't belong to anyone in the neighborhood. (See page 89.)

55

"The wind is cold, and I'm so hungry." *(Photo by Stephanie Rancou, courtesy of the ASPCA Education Dept.)*

Someone may be searching everywhere for his lost pet. If you are positive that your new cat really is a stray and that you may keep him, take him to the veterinarian for an examination and shots just as you did with your first cat.

An adopted kitten should be taken for his shots when he is six weeks old.

Put your new cat in a room by himself. Your first cat will probably stand at the closed door of the room and meow. Cats are jealous of other cats, dogs, and babies. But they can all become friends if their first meetings are handled properly. It's important to avoid shocking either cat by too sudden an introduction.

The first cat should not be ignored because there is a new pet. Give him more attention and affection than before. Let him know that the newcomer will not take his place in your affections or in the house.

To separate cats, a screened or louvered door between rooms is excellent. The two cats are able to see and smell each other without any actual physical contact. If you don't have doors like that, keep the new cat in a separate room with the door closed. Put his own water, food, and litter pan there with him. Take your new cat to the veterinarian before you introduce him to your first cat. The two cats can meet as soon as you know that the new one is healthy.

Getting acquainted should be gradual. Begin by opening the door for a little while every day so the new cat can come out to explore. Your first cat will probably rush into the newcomer's room to sniff everything. Their first meetings shouldn't be more than a half hour, or even less. The new cat may soon want to go back to his room. Take your first cat out if he's there and put your new cat in the room by himself.

Don't be surprised if there are a few hisses and growls from Cat Number One. He's probably expressing fear and resentment, and claiming his rights to territory. Do your best to make him feel better.

Spend time alone with your new pet. Keep bringing him out for longer and longer times each day, but always be present when the two cats are together.

If there are no serious problems after two or three weeks, you can begin leaving them alone together. While they are learning to be friends, they will still need time apart from one another. Every now and then, put the new cat back in his room for a rest.

The building of friendship between two cats takes much longer than people want it to. Most people expect the first and second cats to love each other and play together right away. If this actually happens, consider yourself lucky. It's rare. Cats don't believe in love at first sight. It can be several months before they get used to each other. Be sure that you don't do anything to cause jealousy in either cat.

Some cats become best friends and eat, sleep, and play

Minette (left) was in the house first. She was upset when Sashie came, but later began to wash Sashie and sleep with her. Now they are friends and stay together almost all the time. *(Photo by Marjorie Zaum)*

together, as well as wash each other. Other cats don't pay attention to one another, yet they can live in the same house peacefully for years. Most cats become friends with only a few minor spats every so often.

The second cat will probably not be at all like the first cat. The fun of having more than one cat is that you'll be meeting a new and different personality each time. You'll never be bored!

The introduction of cat and dog can be handled in much the same way. If there is a dog in the house and you're bringing in a cat, the pets will have to be separated from each other at first. The new cat should have his own room where he can go. Make first meetings short. Always be present to supervise each pet.

If the dog chases the cat, you must, of course, stop him. Your cat has no way of knowing that your dog is only playing. A frightened or angry cat can scratch a dog's eyes or nose. If you think your cat is frightened when the dog approaches him, call the dog away.

If you have a cat and are bringing a puppy or grown dog into your house, your cat may be frightened and hide. He may even hiss and growl. Since your cat was in the house first, it's unfair to make him now stay in only one room. In this case, the dog should be shut in for the introductory time. The larger size of a dog is enough to frighten a cat who is not absolutely sure of what the dog is doing. Their noisy, jumpy movements usually make cats nervous. But cats eventually learn that such movements are not threats to them.

With both a dog and a cat in the house, placing the cat's food on the floor can become a problem. Some cats leave food in their

Cats and dogs
can be friends.

dishes to be eaten later. A dog can gulp down a cat's food in a second, so it will have to be kept where the dog can't get it. A kitchen counter, a windowsill, or a table are out of the dog's reach.

A baby gate can be placed in the doorway of any room you don't want the dog to enter. Your cat can go in and out by sliding under the crossbars.

If your cat sleeps with you, don't let a new pet take his place in your bed. Just because the dog is larger, he should never be allowed to take over the cat's toys, his chair, or anything that is specially his, including you. See that your cat's life does not change for the worse because there is a new pet. He should be able to enjoy the new friend, too.

If you give cats and dogs enough time and affection, they can learn to be friends and get along very well.

You may have other pets like hamsters, birds, or fish. The spaces between the bars of cages should be too narrow to allow a cat's paw in. A fishbowl or tank should be covered so he can't poke his paw in the water. Cats are fascinated by the movements of small things; even a moving leaf is very exciting to them. They try to bat or catch anything that moves. This is their nature and it does not mean that they are bad. But your other pets must be protected from cats who will be attracted to their movements.

A new baby is a happy event in everyone's life. The excitement about the new arrival causes some people to forget about their cat or dog. Neglecting your pet at this time might make him jealous of the baby. Show the baby to your cat and let him sniff him or her. He will understand that this is a new, permanent member of the family.

Birds must be protected because cats are attracted to their movements. *(Photo by R.K. Pederson, courtesy of the ASPCA Education Dept.)*

Cats usually like babies and some even climb into cribs and sleep with them. Discourage this, because the baby and the cat may accidentally hurt each other. As the baby grows older, he'll want to play with the cat. Cats usually put up with rougher treatment from babies than they will from older children or adults. Babies like cats because they are soft and warm, but as you know, a cat isn't a stuffed teddy bear. The baby may hurt the cat and the cat may accidentally scratch the baby. They should not be left alone together.

Eventually you can teach your younger brother or sister what you already know—that a cat is not a toy, but has to be cared for and protected.

Sara wants to play with Heidi, the cat, but they are never left alone together. *(Photo courtesy of Hartley and Georgeann Nemerov)*

9
Vacations, Traveling, and Boarding

SCHOOL'S OVER AND IT'S VACATION TIME! THE WEATHER IS beautiful and you and your family are making great plans for a two-week camping trip. You'll be hiking, swimming, and sleeping in a tent.

But wait! What about your cat?

It's not possible to leave your cat alone for more than a day or two. If you're going to be away for more than one night, ask your parents to find a reliable adult friend who will come to the house every day and take care of your cat. The friend must feed him, provide fresh water, and keep the litter pan clean. A person who loves cats will also stay a little while every day to play with him.

Introduce the cat sitter to your cat. Leave enough food for the time you will be gone and show the cat sitter where it is kept. Leave the phone number of your veterinarian. If your cat becomes ill while you're away, the cat sitter can get help.

There are people who walk dogs or take care of cats as a business. Their names, phone numbers, and rates are sometimes listed in the classified section of newspapers. If your parents can't arrange for a friend or neighbor to care for your pet while you're away, they may want to use this service.

Blackberry knows that Allan will take good care of him. *(Photo by Marjorie Zaum)*

Some people want to take their pets with them on vacation. This depends on the type of vacation you are planning. It would be risky to take a pet on a camping trip where the area is unfamiliar to you and might be unsafe for him. But if you're going to stay in one place for a week or two, then it is possible to take your cat, although he probably won't be thrilled with the idea. Call first to make sure that the hotel or the person you're visiting will allow pets!

You must have a cat carrier for traveling. (See page 27.) Whatever type you buy should be large enough for your pet to sit in comfortably. Line it with clean, soft towels and a toy or two. To get him used to it, leave the carrier open so he can explore it before any trips are taken.

You'll have to pack dishes, food, a can opener, litter, litter pan, spoon, and any medicines your cat may be taking. When you arrive, keep him in one room with the doors and windows closed just as you did when he was new in your house.

If you're traveling by car, train, or plane, he should be kept in his carrier during the entire trip. In a car, you can hold the carrier on your lap or put it on the seat next to you. Don't put it on the floor of the car as he may not get enough air. Speak to him in a comforting voice during the trip, as most cats are nervous and frightened when traveling. Some complain very loudly from inside the carrier and some fear traveling so much they even urinate there. A few cats do enjoy traveling and go all over with their owners.

Never leave your cat locked up in a parked car during the hot summer months. The buildup of hot air inside the car can cause him to die from the heat.

If you're traveling by plane, and want to take your pet along, call the airline well in advance of the trip. You will need to know their rules concerning pets and make reservations. A booklet on travel care that you can send away for is listed on page 89.

A cat is happiest in his own home with a friend to care for him, but if no one is available, then you'll have to board him. Some animal hospitals have boarding facilities. Ask your veterinarian to recommend a place. You can also find advertisements for pet boarding in the yellow pages of your phone book.

You and your parents should inspect the boarding place that you choose. The cages should be twice the cat's height, twice his length, and at least three times his width. The litter pans should be clean. The food and water should be clean and fresh. Cat cages should not be facing noisy, barking dogs, as cats can be terrified by these sights and sounds. See if the animals that are there look healthy and clean. If a facility won't let you see the cages, don't board your cat there.

If you must board your cat, do it with sympathy. Remember, he does not know why you are taking him from his home and leaving him in this strange place. Tell him you are coming back for him so that he doesn't feel abandoned.

Whether you have someone in to take care of your pet or board him, the best part of your vacation will be coming home to the friend who has been waiting for you.

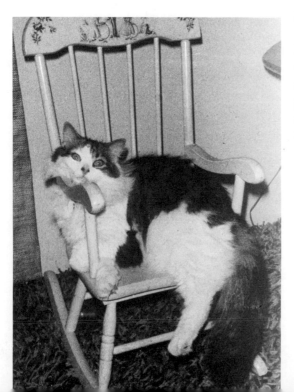

While his owners are away, a cat feels happiest in his own home with a responsible person to care for him.
(Photo by Karen Ault, courtesy of the ASPCA Education Dept.)

10
Your Cat's Body

THE CAT'S BODY CAN BE DESCRIBED AS GRACEFUL AND ELEGANT. In many ways it is similar to the human body. In fact, you and your cat are more alike than you are different.

The human and the cat are both mammals. Both have a four-chambered heart and a circulatory system. Both have eyes, ears, noses, windpipes, and lungs for breathing. They have the same internal organs: stomach, pancreas, liver, kidneys, small intestine, large intestine. Each has a brain and a central nervous system. Each has a reproductive system.

Skeleton. The adult human is about fifteen times the size of the cat, but he has fewer bones. The cat has 230 bones, but the human has only 206.

Nervous system. Your cat is one of the most alert animals on earth. His nervous system quickly sends messages to and from his brain. He can react to things around him faster than most other animals.

The cat's whiskers have nerves at their roots which send

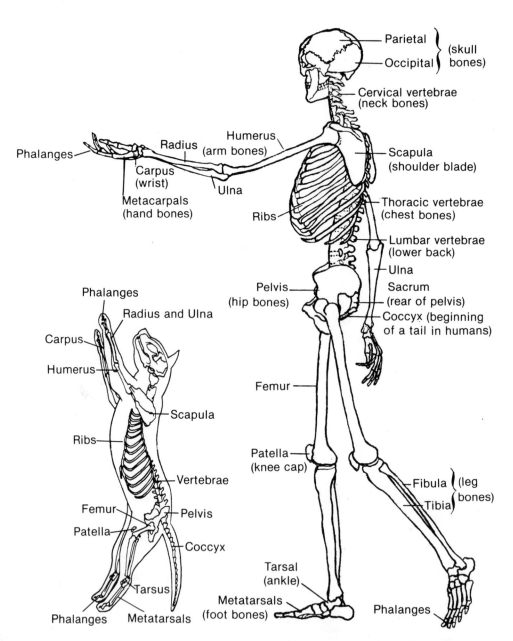

Parietal ⎫ (skull
Occipital ⎬ bones)

Cervical vertebrae
(neck bones)

Humerus
(arm bones)

Radius

Phalanges

Carpus
(wrist)

Ulna

Metacarpals
(hand bones)

Ribs

Scapula
(shoulder blade)

Thoracic vertebrae
(chest bones)

Lumbar vertebrae
(lower back)

Ulna

Pelvis
(hip bones)

Sacrum
(rear of pelvis)

Coccyx (beginning
of a tail in humans)

Femur

Patella
(knee cap)

Fibula ⎫ (leg
Tibia ⎬ bones)

Phalanges

Radius and Ulna

Carpus

Humerus

Scapula

Ribs

Vertebrae

Femur

Pelvis

Patella

Coccyx

Tarsus

Phalanges

Metatarsals

Tarsal
(ankle)

Metatarsals
(foot bones)

Phalanges

The bones of cats are similar to those of humans. Humans even
have the beginnings of a tail, called the coccyx. *(Illustration by Marjorie
Zaum and John D. Loda, D.V.M.)*

messages to the brain. His whiskers help him to touch objects in the darkness and to judge the width of openings through which he may want to crawl.

Reproduction. The cat's reproductive system is like that of humans. But the female cat can only mate at certain times of the year. This is called being *in season* or *in heat*. When in heat, females may call out, roll around, and seem restless. The male cat can mate at any time. If your female cat has mated, kittens will be due in about nine weeks.

The mother-to-be looks for a safe, comfortable place to have

The cat's whiskers help him to "feel" objects in the darkness. *(Photo courtesy of The Humane Society of New York)*

her kittens. When they are born, she washes them. The kittens begin to breathe, but they can't see or hear yet. The mother curls herself around them so they can nurse and be kept warm. Kittens should not be handled during the first week. Mothers and kittens need peace and quiet at this time.

Kittens' eyes begin to open during their second week. They begin crawling around in their box and playing with each other. The mother cat nurses them less and less as they get older. You can start giving them new foods at about three to four weeks. (See the kitten feeding chart on page 35.) At six weeks, the kittens should be taken to a veterinarian for an examination and shots.

Digestive system. The cat's organs of digestion are the same as in humans. But cats, unlike humans, chew their food very briefly and then quickly swallow. Their stomach is very sensitive and they are able to throw up food that is difficult to digest.

Mouth and Teeth. Cats use their lips to hold food in their mouths. Some cats seem to be smiling all the time, but it is doubtful if they can use their lips this way.

The tongue has tiny hooks like a file. The cat uses it to wash and to groom himself by pulling out loose hairs from his coat. The tongue is also used to lap up liquids.

When your cat licks you with his rough little tongue, it may feel as though he's sandpapering your skin. Enjoy it, for it's a compliment. It's one of the ways that cats show their love.

An adult cat has thirty teeth. Kittens cut baby teeth when they're about eleven days old. At three or four months, these teeth are pushed out of the gum to make way for permanent teeth. Cats

If Bootsie loves you, he'll wash you with his rough tongue. *(Photo by Diane Saenz, courtesy of the ASPCA Education Dept.)*

Mooshie's teeth have the same names as human teeth: incisors (the front teeth), canines (the fangs), premolars, and molars. *(Photo by Marjorie Zaum)*

can get gum and tooth problems. They should have their teeth cleaned by a veterinarian about once a year.

Eyes, Ears, and Nose. The beautiful, glowing eyes of the cat have always fascinated people. His eyesight is very sharp. In dim light, the pupils widen to gather in more light. In bright light, the pupils narrow to a thin slit. Cat's eyes glow in the dark because they have an iridescent layer of cells behind the retina. These cells reflect light back through it a second time. This is why cats see so well in dim light.

The cat also has a third eyelid called the *nictitating membrane* which, when closed, lies hidden away in the inner corner of the eye. It is very thin and lets light in, but helps protect the cat's eyes from dust, water, and sharp objects. When it does appear, it is sometimes a sign of illness.

Scientists do not yet know if cats see color. They do know that cats see ultraviolet light, which is a kind of light that humans cannot see. Cats cannot see in total darkness, but their very sensitive whiskers help them to quickly feel their way.

Cats can hear many sounds that humans cannot hear. They can hear high-pitched, faint, and distant sounds, too. Their erect, cupped ears can turn to catch sounds that are coming from different directions.

Someday you may see your cat opening his mouth as though meowing, but no sound comes out. This is called the "silent meow." But is it really silent? Your cat may be speaking to you in a tone so high that you can't hear it!

A healthy cat has a cold, moist nose. He can smell many more odors than humans can. Smell is very important to the cat,

In dim light the pupils widen until they look almost round.
(Photo by Gerald Till, courtesy of the ASPCA Education Dept.)

In bright light the pupils narrow to a thin slit.
(Photo courtesy of The Humane Society of New York)

Sammy turns his ears to catch sounds coming from different directions. *(Photo courtesy of The Humane Society of New York)*

much more so than to humans. You might even say that odors are part of his vocabulary. Let your cat sniff your belongings or something you may be eating. Sniffing new, strange odors is one of the ways your cat learns about the world. A cat will not eat what it cannot smell.

74

Feet and Claws. You may have noticed how softly your cat walks. This is because he walks on his toes, like a ballet dancer. Most cats have five toes on each foot. Under each toe is a soft pad. He has retractable claws enclosed in a sheath and he can extend them or pull them in at will.

He needs his claws for leaping,, gripping surfaces, and for self-defense. They can be used for grasping objects, such as stuffed toys. A cat must scratch to sharpen his claws. It is necessary for his health.

Cats should *not* be declawed. It is painful and inhumane. If your cat scratches furniture, buy or make him a scratching post (see page 24) and patiently train him to use the post, not the furniture, for scratching.

Skin and Hair. The cat's skin, as in humans, consists of two layers, an outer layer and an inner layer. They do not have sweat glands in their skin as humans do. They perspire through their foot pads, nose, and respiratory tract. When a cat pants, he is perspiring through the respiratory tract.

The hair (or fur) grows out of round groups of cells called *follicles* which are buried in the skin. Granules of pigment are deposited in each follicle as the hair grows. This produces the color of a cat's coat.

Your cat is physically like you in many ways. So if you ever wonder how he feels—he feels like you. He can feel hunger and cold, happiness and sadness. Knowing what his body is like will help you to care for him properly.

11
Health Problems

"MY STOMACH HURTS." "I HAVE A SORE THROAT."

Have you ever said that to your parents or to a doctor?

Your cat can't tell you what's wrong with him. When something hurts him, he suffers in silence. It's up to you to watch him and to be alert to any symptoms, or signs of illness.

If you see any of the symptoms listed in this chapter, you and your parents should call your veterinarian immediately. Tell him clearly and accurately what you have seen.

A cat's life span is much shorter than ours. A few days or a week in your life is equal to weeks and months in his. Get medical help quickly if he needs it.

Never try to diagnose and treat your cat yourself. Many diseases have similar symptoms but entirely different methods of treatment. Only a veterinarian, with his medical knowledge and equipment, can tell which illness your cat may have and which medicines he should be given.

Never give your cat any medicine from your home medicine chest. Many drugs which are good for humans are dangerous for cats.

Your cat likes to lead an orderly life, doing the same things every day. Any change in his normal habits means he should be watched carefully.

General Signs of Bad Health
- loss of interest in things
- dull, spiky, or patchy coat
- drinking too much water
- going to the water bowl but unable to drink
- diarrhea
- constipation
- urinating outside the litter pan
- red, watery eyes
- nictitating membrane showing in the inner corner of the eye
- repeated vomiting
- repeated coughing or sneezing
- discharge from eyes or nose
- a lump or swelling

If your cat scratches a lot, he may have *fleas*. Fleas are small insects that live on cats and dogs and feed on their blood. NEVER USE DOG PRODUCTS OR ANYTHING CONTAINING DDT to get rid of fleas on a cat. Ask your veterinarian to recommend a product that is safe for cats. Cats that are kept in the house are not likely to get fleas.

Head shaking, pawing at ears, or ears that look dirty are symptoms of *ear mites*. Ear mites are tiny insects that live in the cat's ear and can cause infections and deafness. See your veterinarian.

Red eyes, coughing, and vomiting are general symptoms of *worms*. Other worm symptoms are: a cat's dragging his rear over the floor, loss of interest in things, loss of weight, pot belly, diarrhea, or constipation. These conditions need a veterinarian's care.

Ringworm is not a worm, but a fungus, which can be transmitted from humans to cats and vice versa. In the cat, the symptom is bald spots in the fur; in you, itchiness, redness, or blotches. You should both have medical treatment, for ringworm is very contagious. It is easy to cure.

Shedding a lot of fur, bald spots around the eyes, or sores and itching are symptoms of a *skin disease*. Medical treatment is needed.

Drooling, bad breath, patting face with paw, and being unable to eat are symptoms of *tooth or gum problems*. Tooth problems are very painful and can cause your pet to stop eating. The infection may spread and become worse. Immediate medical care is needed.

Bleeding, reddened gums, and loss of appetite are symptoms of *gum disease*. Medical care is needed. Blue gums may mean that your cat has been injured and is bleeding internally. See your veterinarian immediately.

Teething in kittens is not a disease, but like babies, they have a hard time. Kittens cut second teeth at three or four months. Sometimes they chew on things like electrical wires. Since this is very dangerous, rub the wires with a bar of soap, which will give them a bad taste. Comfort your kitten and ask your veterinarian what you can give him to chew on while he's teething.

Vomiting is not a disease, but it is a symptom which may be serious. Vomiting a meal right after it is eaten is usually not serious. You can judge if the food was too hot, too cold, or eaten too fast. You can see if your cat has vomited a hairball. If he continues vomiting, or if there are other symptoms, call your veterinarian at once.

Coughing, constipation, refusing food, and vomiting may be symptoms of *hairballs*. Shaped like grayish pieces of rope, they are an accumulation of fur in the cat's stomach or intestine. Since these symptoms are like those of more serious problems, call your veterinarian if they last for more than a day or two. Regular brushing and combing will help to prevent hairballs.

Cats usually go the litter pan once or twice a day. If you see him going to the litter pan many times a day, sitting in the pan, straining, crying, or urinating outside the pan, he may have *cystitis,* a bladder problem. There may be blood in the urine. Cystitis is very painful and serious. CALL YOUR VETERINARIAN IMMEDIATELY.

Extreme thirst, vomiting, and hunching up may be symptoms of *gastritis,* a stomach problem. Since these symptoms are like those of more serious diseases, your cat should have immediate medical attention.

A lump or swelling which increases in size, lack of interest in things, and loss of appetite, may be symptoms of *cancer.* A lump may also be an *abscess.* Your cat should have immediate medical attention.

A high fever, depression, loss of appetite, loss of weight, inability to drink water, vomiting, and diarrhea are symptoms of *feline distemper.* IMMEDIATE MEDICAL ATTENTION IS NEEDED. It is caused by a virus and is the most dreaded of cat diseases. All cats should be inoculated against it. If your veterinarian says that your cat has distemper, you should alert anyone you know who has a cat. Don't visit them and don't let them visit you. The virus is highly contagious. It can be carried on shoes or clothing and be transmitted to other people's cats. Throw away anything your cat has used, such as his litter pan and food dish. When your cat is well, you'll be happy to buy him all new equipment.

Reddened membranes around the eyes, nasal discharge, and sneezing are symptoms of *pneumonitis,* a highly-contagious viral disease. CALL YOUR VETERINARIAN AT ONCE. Friends with cats should be warned. Do not visit each other until your cat is well.

Pot belly is not a disease, but it may be a symptom of worms, a tumor, a uterine infection, or kidney disease. See your veterinarian.

Trembling, vomiting, and fits are symptoms of *poisoning*. SEE YOUR VETERINARIAN AT ONCE. If possible, bring along whatever substance you think has poisoned your cat.

If a female cat rolls on the floor, rubs against objects and people, cries, and seems restless and nervous, she may be *in heat*. Being in heat is not a disease. It is the time when the female cat accepts the male cat for mating and happens most often in spring and summer. Most veterinarians recommend *spaying*. After this operation, your female cat will not be in heat again and she will be unable to have kittens.

Spraying a strong-smelling urine against walls or furniture is done by the mature male cat to attract females and to define, or mark, territory. It is not a disease. Many veterinarians recommend *neutering* when male cats begin to do this. A neutered male cat loses his desire to mate and stops spraying. The odor of his urine is greatly lessened by this operation.

Some cats have problems that are caused by stress. Cats are sensitive and they can get sick if they are very unhappy. Fear, jealousy, or neglect can cause physical illness. Some situations that can upset a cat enough to make him sick are moving to a new house, a new animal in the house whom the cat fears, or a person living in the house who dislikes cats.

81

If your veterinarian tells you that your cat's illness has been caused by stress, you will have to find out why he is so unhappy and try to make things better for him. With medication and understanding, cats recover very quickly.

When you take your cat home after an operation or illness, follow the veterinarian's instructions very carefully. Keep your cat in a warm, quiet room. Don't let other animals or babies annoy him. If you don't have a separate room for him, he can be put in a cage temporarily.

See that he has his medicine, food, water, and litter pan. You can stay with him and talk to him, but don't handle him much. He'll know that you love and care about him.

Cats are healthy and strong in spite of the problems listed in this chapter. Most house cats live their entire lives without a single serious illness, and no cat gets everything all at once! The problems listed in this chapter can all be cured if caught early enough, so be an alert cat owner.

12
Nobody Wants Me

"GET RID OF THAT CAT." HOW OFTEN PEOPLE SAY THAT! But a cat is not a piece of garbage. Garbage is gotten rid of—not living, breathing, feeling animals. Only the most uncaring people speak this way. Usually they are the same ones who allow their cats to roam freely and produce litter after litter of unwanted kittens. Then they refuse the responsibility of taking care of the kittens whose lives they regard as worthless.

The Humane Society of the United States reports that, nationwide, over eight million kittens and cats are collected or turned in each year, and only 9.1 percent are reclaimed or adopted. This means that over 90 percent of the animals brought to shelters are put to death. This figure does not include the thousands and thousands of sick and miserable strays that roam the streets.

If the time comes when, for some reason, you are unable to keep your pet, try the best you can to place him with a kind person or family. Do not give him to another child unless his parents agree to take your cat. Ask adult friends, relatives, and neighbors. Ask your parents to place an ad in your local newspaper and put up notices in local stores offering your cat for adoption. Don't give

IT'S MORE THAN CRUEL TO ABANDON AN ANIMAL. IT'S AGAINST THE LAW.

NEW YORK STATE LAW:

Abandonment of animals

A person being the owner or possessor, or having charge or custody of an animal, who abandons such animal, or leaves it to die in a street, road or public place, or who allows such animal, if it becomes disabled, to lie in a public street, road or public place more than three hours after he receives notice that it is left disabled, is guilty of a misdemeanor, punishable by imprisonment for not more than one year, or by a fine of not more than $500, or by both.

This public service brought to you by Bide-a-Wee Home Association.

PHOTOGRAPHS BY MICHEL TCHEREVKOFF

(Courtesy of the Bide-A-Wee Home Association)

up and don't abandon him to the street. If, after really trying, you can't find anyone to give your cat a home, take him to your local humane society.

Each kitten and cat is a spark of life and deserves the best that life has to offer—not pain, suffering, and starvation. Anyone who wants a kitten or cat should adopt one from an animal shelter. A cat adopted from an animal shelter is just as beautiful, as lovable, and as fine a companion as any fancy breed bought from an expensive pet shop.

Don't allow more kittens to be born unless you and your family are willing and able to take care of all of them and their descendants for the rest of their lives. Most veterinarians recommend the neutering of males and the spaying of females to prevent unwanted kittens from being born. Hopefully, veterinary

The animals are being adopted from the Bide-A-Wee Shelter in New York. *(Bide-A-Wee photo by Susan Brooks)*

medicine will some day soon develop simpler solutions in the form of safe birth control drugs for animals.

If you find a stray cat, make absolutely sure he's not somebody's lost pet. Once they get over their terror and are given a home, good food, and care, stray cats become the most loving and devoted of pets. If your parents won't allow you to keep him, ask them to help you bring him to a shelter. He will be better off there than on the street. Remember, if you don't care, no one else will. You can't assume that somebody else will take care of the cat you walk away from.

The condition of animals all over the world is tragic. Certain species are becoming extinct because of the selfishness and cruelty of many human beings. Young people can help to change this terrible situation. If you are a young person who is kind to animals, you will grow up to be an adult who is kind to animals and people alike.

(Photo courtesy of The Humane Society of New York)

# Publications About Cats

You can send away for these informative publications about cats. They are all free.

Poisonous Plants
The Humane Society of the United States
2100 L Street, N.W.
Washington, D.C. 20037
    Ask for: *Poisonous Plants That Can Hurt Your Pet*

Allergy Problem
Send a stamped, self-addressed envelope to:
Allergy Problem
c/o Associated Humane Societies
P.O. Box 200
Keyport, New Jersey 07735

Cat Care
The Humane Society of the United States
2100 L Street, N.W.
Washington, D.C. 20037
    Ask for: *The Kind Report: Caring for Your Cat*

Send a stamped, self-addressed envelope to:
ASPCA
441 East 92 Street
New York, New York 10028
    Ask for: *Care for Cats Information Bulletin*

Adopting a Cat
Send a stamped, self-addressed envelope to:
ASPCA
441 East 92 Street
New York, New York 10028
    Ask for: *Thinking of Adopting A Cat Information Bulletin*

Clues About Cats
Send a stamped, self-addressed envelope to:
Pioneers for Animal Welfare Society (PAWS)
Box 861
Hicksville, New York 11802
    Ask for:*Clues About Cats*

Traveling
Send a stamped, self-addressed envelope to:
Travel With Pet Guidelines
Bide-A-Wee Association
410 East 38th Street
New York, New York 10016

Lost and Found
Send a stamped, self-addressed envelope to:
Pioneers for Animal Welfare Society (PAWS)
Box A-485
Wantagh, New York 11793
    Ask for: *Lost and Found Directory*

Helping Animals
Send a stamped, self-addressed envelope to:
Pioneers for Animal Welfare Society (PAWS)
Box 861
Hicksville, New York 11802
    Ask for: *Helping Animals: A Young Person's Guide to
        Animal Protection*

For Teachers
Teachers can receive information about *The Humane Education
Program in Schools* by sending a stamped, self-addressed,
legal-size envelope to:
Pioneers for Animal Welfare Society (PAWS)
Box 861
Hicksville, New York 11802

Poisonous Plants

This is a partial list of plants that are poisonous to pets.

Plant	Poisonous Parts	Plant Type
apple	seeds	cultivated tree
azaleas	entire plant	cultivated and wild shrub
caladium	entire plant	house plant
castor bean	entire plant	house plant
Christmas rose	rootstock, leaves	garden flower
daffodil	bulbs	garden flower
dumb cane	entire plant	house plant
elephant's ear	entire plant	house plant
English ivy	entire plant, especially leaves and berries	ornamental vine
foxglove	leaves	wild and garden flower
holly	berries	shrub
horse chestnut	nuts, sprouts	tree
hyacinth	bulbs	wild and house plant
iris	leaves, roots	wild and garden flower
lantana	foliage	house plant
laurel	leaves	shrub
lily of the valley	leaves, flowers	garden and wild flower
mistletoe	berries	house plant
narcissus	bulbs	garden flower
oak	shoots, leaves	tree
philodendron	entire plant	house plant
poinsettia	leaves, stem, flowers	house plant
potato	shoots, sprouts	garden plant
rhododendron	leaves	ornamental shrub
wisteria	pods, seeds	ornamental plant

Some Common Household Substances Poisonous to Cats

house paint
turpentine and varnish
artist's oil paints
flea powder and spray for dogs
strong detergents
insecticides, either sprays or powders
zinc ointment
disinfectants or cleaners* that contain *phenol*
     (carbolic acid)
clorox
laundry bleach
roach poison
rat poison
plant sprays
plant fertilizers
paint remover
nail polish remover
DDT
kerosene
calamine lotion
coolant (used in cars)

Pine oil disinfectants in a diluted solution (1 part disinfectant to 5 parts water) are considered adequate for cleaning and safe for cats.

> If you suspect that your cat has swallowed poison, SEE A VETERINARIAN IMMEDIATELY.

Glossary

Abscess An inflamed sore—it can appear anywhere on the body.

Ash content The leftover part of food after the body has used all that it can.

Board To leave your pet in a special place or kennel where it will be cared for while you are away.

Body language Body positions or gestures which express meaning.

Cancer A disease sometimes characterized by a tumor that keeps on growing; at other times, as in cat leukemia (loo-keem-ee-uh), it is a blood disease.

Carnivorous Meat-eating.

Carrier or carrying case A fiberboard or heavy cardboard container with air holes. It is used for transporting cats.

Catnip An aromatic plant which attracts cats. Chewing the leaves makes them feel excited. The plant is a member of the mint family and is sometimes called catmint.

Circulatory system The system of tube-like structures by which the blood is moved through the body.

Diagnosis The process of identifying a disease by examination.

Diarrhea A loose bowel movement.

Digestive system The system of structures that transforms food into simpler substances that the body can use.

Dilute Mix with water.

Dinictis An ancestor of today's cat, believed to have lived about thirty million years ago.

Domestic pet House pet.

Ear mites Tiny insects that sometimes infest ears of cats, causing them to constantly scratch themselves.

Embalm To prevent the decay of a corpse by treatment with preservatives.

ESP Stands for "extra sensory perception" which means being aware of people, things or animals, events, etc. through senses other than the normal ones of sight, hearing, taste, smell, and touch.

Extinct No longer existing in living form as a group or kind of living thing—died out.

Feline distemper Also called feline panleukopenia (pan-loo-koh-pen-ee-uh), a contagious viral disease with symptoms of high fever, loss of appetite, vomiting, and weakness.

Felis The scientific name of our present day cat.

Fleas Small insects that live on cats and dogs and feed on their blood.

Follicles Round groups of cells in which hairs are rooted.

Furballs See hairballs.

Gastritis A stomach disorder—may be a symptom of a serious infectious disease or poisoning.

Groom To brush or comb loose hairs from your cat's coat. Cats groom themselves, too, by washing themselves with their tongues.

Hairballs An accumulation of loose hairs in the stomach or intestine of the cat

Humane Society An organization that shelters homeless animals. Some have medical clinics and some offer animals for adoption.

Inflammation Localized heat, swelling, and pain due to irritation, injury, or infection.

In heat A regularly recurring period of ovulation in female mammals other than humans. Also known as in season or estrus.

Knead The pushing up and down of the cat's front paws against soft things or on the lap of a person it loves. The motion is probably connected to the way a kitten nurses against its mother's side.

Litter Ground clay which is very absorbent and is used in pans for the cat's toilet.

Litter (of kittens) The young produced at one birth.

Litter pan or tray Usually a plastic pan, at least 18 inches long and 14 inches wide, with sides 3 inches high, that is used for the cat's toilet.

Miacis Early ancestor of the cat.

Mummify To make ready for burial by embalming in the ancient Egyptian way.

Neuter A surgical operation on male cats which causes them to lose interest in mating with females.

Nictitating membrane An extra eyelid. All cats have a pair of them.

Nocturnal Active at night.

Pneumonitis (new-mon-eye-tis) A viral disease of the lungs and upper respiratory tract.

Pot belly The condition of a swollen or enlarged midsection of a cat. It is not a disease but may be the symptom of a tumor or other disease.

Retina The light-sensitive membrane lining the inner eyeball.

Retractable Capable of being extended or pulled in.

Scratching post A log or piece of wood covered with bark or carpet and attached to a strong base.

Spay An operation to remove the ovaries and uterus of the female cat who will then be unable to have kittens.

Spray The unaltered male cat sprays urine on walls or furniture to attract females and to define territory. Sometimes females in heat also do this.

Treat Any food which is good for cats but is not a regular part of their diets.

Tumor A lump or mass that may appear on any part of the cat's body, inside or outside, and may either grow quickly to become a dangerous cancer, may not grow at all, or may even disappear after awhile.

Ultraviolet light Light which is beyond violet in the color spectrum and which humans cannot see.

Veterinarian A medical doctor who specializes in treating domestic animals.

Vibration A rapid back and forth motion.

Worms Parasites that sometimes infest cats.

Index